Dedicated with love
to our own children...
...and to all the children of the world!

Shelly and Melissa Frase

Susan Jeff and Krista Hunt

Kurt Lynn and Suzy Liebert

all the children of the world

Loaves and Fishes

A "Love Your Neighbor" Cookbook

Linda Hunt
Marianne Frase
Doris Liebert

HERALD PRESS

Scottdale, Pennsylvania
Kitchener, Ontario

Library of Congress Cataloging in Publication Data

Hunt, Linda, 1940-
    Loaves and Fishes.

    Includes index.
    SUMMARY: a cookbook emphasizing eating one's fair
share of healthful food in a world of limited   resources. Includes about 120 recipes.
    1.   Cookery -- Juvenile literature   2. Cookery
(Natural foods) -- Juvenile literature [1. Cookery
-- Natural foods] I. Frase, Marianne, 1935-
joint author. II. Liebert, Doris, date- joint
author. III. Title.
TX652.5.H86   641.5'637   80-12165
ISBN   0-8361-1922-3 (pbk.)

LOAVES AND FISHES

Library of Congress Catalog Card Number: 80-12165
International Standard Book Number: 0-8361-1922-3
Printed in the United States of America

15 14 13 12 11 10 9 8 7 6 5

Contents

Loaves and Fishes

(a cookbook for kids who care)

Let me tell you a true story...

about

...a young boy who
shared a small gift
that became the
makings of a miracle!

Once upon a time...
near the Sea of Galilee, a young boy
followed a huge crowd that had gathered
to see and hear Jesus. They had heard
of the wonderful things He had done
to help people and
wanted to know more. They
stopped to rest on a
grassy hillside and
it was here that
the "magnificent
miracle" happened!

When Jesus arrived, He looked
at the five thousand people waiting for Him.
He knew that they were tired and hungry,
for they had traveled a long way!

...and He cared about that!

He asked His
disciples, Philip and Andrew,
"How can we feed all these people?"

The disciples felt this would be
impossible. It would take a great deal of
money to buy food for so many!

At this time the young boy offered his picnic basket to Andrew. It was only a simple lunch of five barley loaves and two little fishes.

Andrew wondered to himself, "What good is this when so many are hungry?"

But he took the boy's basket to Jesus anyway.

John 6:1-14

    Jesus, however, was very happy with the small gift and with the boy who had wanted to share it. He knew just what He was going to do!

    Asking the crowd to sit down, He took the loaves and the fishes and thanked God for the child's generous gift.

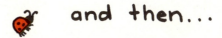 and then...

...the miracle happened!

     Jesus passed the basket to the people and the one little lunch grew and grew so that all who were there were able to eat as much as they wanted until they were full!

Can you imagine feeding all the kids in your school (and more) from just <u>your</u> lunchbox?!

There were even leftovers! And Jesus told the disciples to collect the food that was left so nothing would be wasted. It took <u>12</u> baskets to carry what was not eaten! Everyone was <u>AMAZED</u> ... especially the boy! Amazing! What a celebration!

Amazing! Amazing!

That happened a long time ago, but Jesus still cares that everyone in the world has enough to eat.

As with the gift of the young boy's lunch, what we do with our food can make a difference!

It's true!
Look on the next pages for some important facts...

If all the children in the whole world came to a party to share one GIGANTIC cake, North American children would receive more than a fair share of it.

Hey, kids — and Moms and Dads! You can find official statistics on world food consumption in the book The Twenty-Ninth Day by Lester Brown.

Not only do some of the world's children miss out on birthday cake,

they don't get enough healthy mealtime foods either.

Grains Consumed Yearly

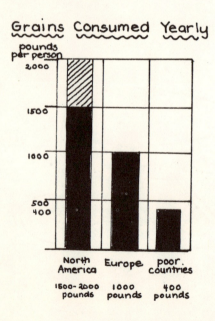

pounds per person

North America	1500-2000 pounds
Europe	1000 pounds
poor countries	400 pounds

As this graph shows, the average North American uses 4-5 times more grain per person each year than does one of the two billion persons living in poor countries. The major reason for the glaring difference in the height of the columns is that much of North America's grain is consumed indirectly through grain-fed animals (livestock and fowl).

Unfortunately, it's not just the cake and treats...

but it's meat, eggs, fruit, and milk too-- all the world's foods.

What can we do about it?

We can become discouraged and feel
helpless as Andrew and Philip did looking
at the crowd needing to eat —

 or...

We can follow the example of the young boy.
He came forward with a small offering even
though the situation seemed hopeless.

   The story shows how Jesus can use our
little efforts to help solve giant problems.

With Jesus' touch —
little is much!

Let's look at some of these efforts we can make... some steps we can take!

1st ... <u>awareness</u>! As children, we can become AWARE.... We know we can't solve the world's food problem. Many grown-ups are working on that. But we can learn of food needs in other nations. So watch the news on television, read the newspaper, study other countries in school.

2nd ... <u>research</u>! We can check our school lunch program for nutrition and waste.

3rd 👣 ... <u>choices</u>! We can start within ourselves and in our families, choosing to eat and cook more carefully!

This means choosing foods that are good for us and that use less energy ...

...to grow,

...to process,

...and prepare.

And also
learning to eat what our bodies need without being wasteful.

Wouldn't that be fairer for everyone?

Remember in our story that Jesus didn't want anything to be wasted. We can be especially careful about this!

Take only what you know you can eat so nothing will be thrown away!

Also the crowd was satisfied with the boy's simple lunch.

The Bible says they had enough.

Many of us in North America don't lack food, but we don't choose the best kinds of food because we don't know which ones are best for healthy growth.

By learning to cook and enjoy simple health-giving foods, we are taking a beginning step toward using the world's limited resources wisely.

Hey! We _can_ do something!

Sooo...

... here's a special cookbook,

Loaves and Fishes —

for kids who care!

Let's Cook!

Cooking Tools

for measuring and preparing...

mixing bowls

measuring cups

grater

mixer

measuring spoons

mixing spoon

knife

parer

cutting board

hand beater

blender

whipper

strainer

rolling pin

...for cooking and baking...

saucepan

loaf pan

skillet

baking pans

baking sheet

...and
for safety's sake...
always turn pot and
pan handles toward
the back of stove
and ALWAYS use
pot holders

cookie cutters

muffin pan

and hot pads.

Cooking Tips

Before You Cook

Check to see that it's okay to use the kitchen.
Read through the entire recipe and gather all ingredients
and tools.
Wash your hands and you're ready to cook.

While You Cook

Measure ingredients carefully and cook according to directions.
Get help with beaters, blenders, and chopping if needed.
Keep pot holders handy for hot pans, and sponges for spills.
Dry your hands before you plug or unplug appliances.
Set timer or watch the clock.
Always turn handles to back of stove to avoid spills.

After You Cook

Turn off the stove and unplug appliances.
Return ingredients to their places and leave kitchen clean
for next cook.

I'd like that!
I'll be next!

Cooking Terms

Blend and mix-- Mix 2 or more ingredients until smooth.

Beat-- Mix vigorously by hand or electric mixer.

Boil-- Heat mixture in saucepan until bubbles form on top.

Whip-- Beat rapidly with a spoon, whisk, or electric beater.

Grate-- Rub ingredients across grater to cut into small pieces.

Simmer-- Cook food on top of stove at a very low heat. Tiny bubbles will form around edge of pan.

Chop or mince-- Cut with knife to make small pieces.

Broil-- Cook food on top rack of oven in a broiler pan. Put oven knob on <u>Broil</u>.

Bake-- Cook food in oven. (Be sure to set temperature knob!)

Grease-- Spread bottom and sides of pan with shortening or margarine.

Dot-- Put small portions of shortening or margarine on a given area.

Snacks and Garden Goodies

34

Ladybug Salad

What You Need:

½ ripe tomato
black olives (sliced)
celery "feathers"
toothpicks

What You Get:

A salad that looks
just like me! →
Wow!

...named after me!
You know it _has_ to be good!

What You Do:

1. Place tomato half on plate so rounded side is up.

2. Use toothpicks to place olives on tomato to make the ladybug's head and spots.

3. Use the leafy ends of the celery (the "feathers") to make the antennae.

Strawberry Freezer Pops

What You Need:

2 cups strawberries
(washed and cut up)
2 cups buttermilk
¾ cup sugar

popsicle molds

What You Get:

A cool fruity treat
for a warm day!

Be sure to ask for
some help before using
the blender!

What You Do:

1. Place all ingredients in blender jar. Blend only until mixed. (Or use mixer.)
2. Pour mixture into popsicle molds.
3. Place in freezer until hard.
4. Take out of freezer a few minutes before removing from mold.
5. Eat and enjoy!

Sunflower - Cheese Treats

What You Need:

```
1 package cream cheese
    (8 ounces)
1 small bag sunflower seeds
    (shelled)
soy sauce
assorted crackers
    (Triscuits, Wheat Thins)
```

What You Get:

Another great snack you will want to fix often!

I LOVE sunflower seeds!

What You Do:

1. Sprinkle and press sunflower seeds into top of cream cheese block.
2. Pour a few drops of soy sauce on top of cheese and seeds.
3. Slice small amount and place on top of crackers.

Great Granola

What You Need:

8 cups rolled oats
1 cup flaked coconut
1 cup sesame seeds
1 cup chopped almonds
1 cup raw wheat germ
½ cup sunflower seeds
½ cup chopped nuts
   (any kind you like)
½ cup chopped dates, raisins
   (or any dried fruit you like)

sauce: ¾ cup honey
   ½ cup peanut butter
   ¼ cup vegetable oil
   ⅓ cup water
   ½ teaspoon cinnamon

a very large bowl
3 or 4 large shallow pans
large storage tin or jar
   (with tight cover)

Great Granola

This basic granola mix is great! Eat it plain or look on page 40 for some more ideas of what you can do with granola! Yum!

What You Do:

1. In a very large bowl stir together the oats, coconut, wheat germ, nuts, sesame and sunflower seeds.

2. In a saucepan heat together all of the sauce ingredients — honey, peanut butter, oil, water, and cinnamon.

3. Pour heated sauce over dry ingredients and stir well.

4. Spread mixture into shallow pans.

5. Bake at 375° about 15 minutes.

6. Let mixture cool in pans. Then pour it into large bowl once again and add dried fruit you have chosen.

7. Store your great granola mix in a jar.

What You Get:

about 4 pounds of granola for nibbling or...

look at next page

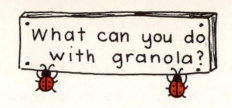

What can you do with granola?

1. Eat as cereal at breakfast time (or anytime). Just pour on milk and enjoy!

...or 2. It makes a great nibble food for an after-school snack or to take along on your next hiking or bike trip. It's also easy to carry to the ball game. Try it!

... or 3. Sprinkle it over fruit, pudding, or yogurt.

or even ice cream!

4. Use it to make Great Granola Cookies. Look on the next page for the recipe...

Great Granola Cookies

Great to eat and great for you!

What You Need:

1 cup shortening
½ cup brown sugar
½ cup granulated sugar
2 eggs
1 teaspoon vanilla
½ cup whole wheat flour
1 cup unbleached flour
1 teaspoon salt
1 teaspoon baking soda
1 cup rolled oats
2 cups Great Granola
   (see page 38)

large bowl
cookie sheet

What You Do:

1. In large bowl beat shortening and sugars until smooth and creamy.

2. Add eggs and vanilla. Mix well.

3. Add flours, salt, and baking soda, and continue beating until well mixed.

4. Stir in the oats and granola. (Look back on page 38 for Great Granola mix.)

5. Grease cookie sheet and drop mix by teaspoonfuls. Bake at 350° for about 12 minutes.

What You Get:

About 6 dozen cookies!

Banana Split Salad

What You Need:

> 1 banana
> 1 or 2 scoops cottage cheese
> your choice of fruits
>   and nuts you like too
>
>   some imagination
>   a bowl or fancy dish

What You Get:

A chance to use your creativity and to eat a delicious salad treat!

Scatter nuts over it all if you like or yogurt fans can spoon a little on top! Yum!

What You Do:

1. Cut the banana in half lengthwise and put in a dish or bowl.

2. Top the banana with a scoop or 2 of cottage cheese.

3. Now! Use your imagination and top the cottage cheese with any of your favorite cut-up fruits.

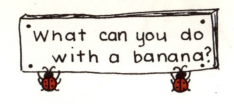

What can you do with a banana?

1. Make Frozen Bananas

Peel, cut in half, and put a popsicle stick in end. Cover with plastic wrap and freeze.

or 3. Banana Split Salad

← (See opposite page.)

and 4. Christmas Candle Fruit Salad

(See page 102.)

or 2. Baked Bananas

Peel, cut in half, and then in half again (lengthwise). Dot with margarine or butter, sprinkle with sugar and cinnamon. Bake at 350° for 15-20 minutes.

5. Banana-Nut Birthday Cake

(See page 77.)

Spokane's Riverfront Park

Jeff's Jiffy "Cracker Jacks"

What You Need:

```
¼ cup margarine or butter
½ cup honey
6 cups popped corn
1 cup peanuts
    popcorn popper
    very large bowl
    saucepan
2 large shallow pans
```

What You Get:

"Cracker Jacks" just like you buy at the park!

What You Do:

1. In saucepan heat over low heat the honey and margarine just until blended.

2. In large bowl mix popcorn and peanuts. Add sauce and stir.

3. Spread mixture into 2 large pans.

4. Bake at 350° for 7-10 minutes.

5. When cool, stir, and it's ready to eat!

Graham Crackers

What You Need:

½ cup margarine
⅔ cup brown sugar
½ cup water
2¾ cups graham flour
½ teaspoon salt
½ teaspoon baking powder
⅛ teaspoon cinnamon

large bowl
rolling pin
cookie cutters
cookie sheet

What You Do:

1. In large bowl put margarine and sugar. Beat until smooth and creamy.

2. Add the rest of the ingredients to the margarine-sugar mixture and mix well.

3. Let the mixture sit for 30-45 minutes.

What You Get:

Your own "homemade" graham crackers!

Imagine that!

4. Sprinkle some flour on a bread board or a tabletop and then roll out the dough about 1/8 inch thick.

5. Cut with cutters into squares, logs, or whatever shape you would like and place on oiled cookie sheet.

6. Bake at 350° for 20 minutes until lightly brown.

Especially good with hot cocoa on a cold winter's day!.

Carob Candy Squares

What You Need:

½ cup peanut butter (creamy)
½ cup honey
½ cup unsweetened carob powder
       or cocoa
½ cup sunflower seeds
½ cup roasted soybeans, dry-roasted
    peanuts, or Spanish peanuts
½ cup raisins or cut-up dates
½ cup flaked coconut
2 Tablespoons wheat germ
and then another ½ cup coconut

saucepan
loaf pan
wax paper

What You Do:

1. In saucepan heat the honey and peanut butter just until melted.

2. Remove from heat and stir in the carob powder just until blended.

3. Stir in sunflower seeds, soybeans or nuts, fruit, and

½ cup of the coconut.

4. Place a lining of wax paper into a loaf pan and press carob mixture into pan.

5. Sprinkle the remaining ½ cup of coconut over the top. Press it lightly into mixture.

6. Cover pan and put it into refrigerator until the candy is chilled and firm.

7. Cut into squares to serve. Keep it covered in the refrigerator (if it isn't eaten up right away!).

<u>What</u> <u>You</u> <u>Get:</u>

About 24 pieces of "candy" that's yummy in the tummy!

It's yummy in the tummy!

Soft Whole Wheat Pretzels

What You Need:

2 loaves frozen whole
  wheat bread
1 egg white, slightly beaten
1 teaspoon water
coarse salt

  baking sheet
  small bowl
  pastry brush
  pan with water

What You Get:

2 dozen pretzels you'll
have fun baking!

What You Do:

1. Thaw frozen loaves of dough in the refrigerator overnight.

2. Divide each thawed loaf into 12 balls.

3. Roll each ball into a rope 12 inches long.

4. Shape dough into pretzels by forming a knot and looping ends through.

5. Grease baking sheet and place the pretzels 1 inch apart.

6. In small bowl combine egg whites and water. Brush on pretzels and sprinkle coarse salt on top.

7. In large shallow pan pour 1 inch of hot water and place it on the very bottom rack of the oven.

8. Place the pretzels on the middle rack of the oven and bake at 350° for 20 minutes.

Healthy snacks give you energy for after-school sports!

Munch... crunch!

Munchkin Crunchkins

What You Need:

1 cup margarine (2 sticks)
3/4 cup brown sugar
3/4 cup white sugar
2 eggs
1 teaspoon vanilla
2 cups unbleached flour
1/2 teaspoon baking powder
1 teaspoon soda
1/2 teaspoon salt
1/4 cup raw wheat germ
2 cups rolled oats
3 cups Special K cereal
1 cup coconut
1 cup pecans, or walnuts

large mixing bowl
cookie sheet

What You Do:

1. In large bowl beat together the margarine and sugars until creamy.

2. Add eggs and vanilla. Mix well.

3. Add flour, baking powder, soda, salt, and wheat germ. Mix well.

4. Add oats, cereal, coconut, and nuts. Mix until well blended.

5. Drop by teaspoonfuls on ungreased cookie sheet.

6. Bake at 350° for 8-10 minutes.

What You Get:

6-8 dozen cookies.

Cheese – Dates

What You Need:

> 1 3-ounce package cream cheese
> ½ cup finely chopped walnuts
> pitted dates

What You Get:

2 – 3 dozen naturally sweet treats!

What You Do:

1. Soften cream cheese by taking it out of refrigerator an hour ahead.

2. Mix cream cheese with nuts.

3. Fill pitted sliced dates with 1 teaspoon cheese mixture.

what fun!

Suzy's Peanut-Butter Play Dough

What You Need:

½ cup peanut butter
¼ cup honey
1 cup dry milk solids

mixing bowl
rolling pin
cookie cutters
and
some creativity

What You Get:

Play dough you can eat!

What You Do:

1. In bowl mix peanut butter, honey, and ½ cup dry milk with your hands.

2. Keep adding rest of dry milk until dough feels soft and playful.

3. Shape in any form you like or roll it out and cut into shapes with cookie cutters. Add raisins to decorate.

Quick 'n Crazy Carob Cake

What You Need:

1½ cups unbleached flour
¾ cup sugar
1 teaspoon salt
1 teaspoon soda
4 teaspoons carob powder
    or cocoa
6 Tablespoons vegetable oil
1 Tablespoon vinegar
1 teaspoon vanilla
½ teaspoon cinnamon
1 cup water

8" x 8" square baking pan

What You Do:

1. In square baking pan stir together the flour, sugar, salt, soda, and carob powder.

2. With a spoon make 3 wells or holes in the dry ingredients.

3. In one hole put the oil, in another the vinegar, and in the other the vanilla.

4. Pour water over it all and stir until thoroughly mixed.

5. Bake at 375° for 25 minutes.

What You Get:

A deliciously easy cake to bake - it's quick and has no messy bowls to wash!

Hooray!

Krista's Cucumber Coins

What You Need:

> 1 cucumber
> cottage cheese
> parsley
> seasoned salt

What You Do:

1. Carefully slice cucumbers in rounds on a wooden cutting board.

2. Frost with cottage cheese.

3. Sprinkle with salt and parsley.

What You Get:

A crunchy snack!

Krista's coins are colossal!

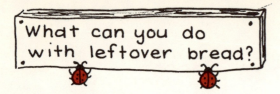

What can you do with leftover bread?

Use up the bits and pieces— some "no-waste" ideas!

1. Make Rusks

Spread stale bread or toast on baking sheet. Bake at 275° for 1 hour. (It's a chewy treat for baby brother or sister!)

or 2. Make Croutons

Cut up bread in cubes. Bake according to Rusk recipe and sprinkle with garlic salt or Parmesan cheese. You may want to melt a little butter or margarine in pan to coat cubes. (Great for soups and salads!)

or 3. Cheese Cubes

If you have leftover grilled cheese sandwiches, cut them in cubes, toast as in Rusk recipe. Use as croutons or bite-sized nibbles.

4. Make Viennese Beggarman's Pudding (See page 151.)

5. Marvelous Meat Loaf (See page 87.)

Apple Crisp

What You Need:

4 apples
3/4 cup rolled oats
1/2 cup brown sugar
1/2 cup unbleached flour
1 teaspoon cinnamon
1/2 cup margarine
small bowl
square baking pan
8" x 8"

What You Do:

1. Peel apples and then slice.
2. Spread apples in 8" x 8" pan.
3. In small bowl combine the rest of the ingredients, then sprinkle over apples.
4. Bake at 350° for 35 - 40 minutes.
5. Serve warm or cold!

What You Get:
6 servings of a crispy apple treat! Delicious anytime!

Acorn Squash Boats

What You Need:

> 2 acorn squash
> (cut in half)
> 1 cup applesauce
> ½ teaspoon cinnamon
> ~
> large shallow pan
> water

What You Do:

1. Cut squash in half. (You might need to ask for some help with this.)

2. Scoop out the seeds with a spoon and then place squash in a baking dish with the cut side down.

Be sure to save the seeds to make "Birdseed" Snacks (see page 65).

...and then...

3. Add enough water to fill ½ inch.

4. Bake at 400° for 25 minutes.

5. Carefully remove pan from oven with pot holders and set on a hot pad.

6. Turn squash right side up and fill center holes with applesauce. Sprinkle cinnamon over top.

7. Return pan to oven and bake 20-25 minutes more or until tender when pierced with a fork.

<u>What</u> <u>You</u> <u>Get</u>:

4 squash boats - a festive fall treat from the garden!

Make-Ahead Muffin Mix

What You Need:

3 cups All-Bran cereal
1 cup boiling water
2 eggs
2 cups buttermilk
½ cup vegetable oil
1 cup chopped dates or
   raisins
2½ teaspoons soda
½ teaspoon salt
1 cup sugar
2 Tablespoons raw wheat
   germ
2½ cups unbleached flour

large bowl
muffin pans
cupcake papers

What You Do:

1. In large bowl, mix Bran cereal and boiling water.

2. In a cup, beat the eggs a little with a fork. Add to Bran mix along with buttermilk, oil, and fruit.

3. Stir well and then add the soda, salt, sugar, wheat germ, and flour. Mix well.

You are now ready to bake the mix — or store until later. Look on next page...

4. Batter can be baked now or can be stored in a covered jar up to 2 weeks.

5. When you wish to bake some muffins, put cupcake papers in muffin tins. Fill about ⅔ full.

6. Bake at 425° for about 20 minutes.

What You Get:

Batter for about 2½ dozen muffins that can be ready to bake in a minute!

Nuts and Bolts

What You Need:

1 cup spoon-size shredded wheat
1 cup Wheat Chex
1 cup Cheerios
1 Tablespoon vegetable oil
1 teaspoon seasoned salt
2/3 cup toasted Spanish
    peanuts or soybeans
large skillet

What You Do:

1. In large skillet pour oil, turn stove burner to low. Add 3 cereals and stir until lightly toasted.

2. Sprinkle with salt.

3. Remove carefully from stove — add peanuts or soybeans. Store in a jar with a tight lid.

What You Get:

A delicious after-school snack or special gift to give to friends...

"Birdseed" Snacks

It's really for kids—
not the birds!

What You Need:

2 cups pumpkin or
    squash seeds

2 Tablespoons margarine,
         melted

salt

strainer
small saucepan
cookie sheet

What You Get:

2 cups of nibbles — just
perfect to carry along
on your next bike ride or hike!

What You Do:

1. Save pumpkin and squash seeds until you have about 2 cups.

2. Use strainer to rinse and drain the seeds. Pat dry in paper towel.

3. In saucepan melt margarine. Stir seeds into margarine.

4. Spread seeds on cookie sheet. Sprinkle with salt.

5. Bake at 350° for about 30 minutes or until nearly dry.

Build-Your-Own Soup

It's a soup party! Fun to do and nutritious too!

What You Need:

2 cans chicken broth
   or beef broth
1 cup cooked chicken, chopped
   (or other leftover meat)
2 cups finely chopped vegetables
   (of your choice)   carrots,
                broccoli,
                cauliflower,
   or cooked leftovers such as
                green beans,
                corn,
                etc.
2 cups cubed cheese —
   swiss, cheddar, or jack
parsley and Parmesan cheese

   saucepan,
   lazy susan, or
   several small bowls

What You Do:

1. In saucepan heat broth.

2. On cutting board chop meat and vegetables of your choice. Cut up cheese in small cubes.

3. Arrange each vegie, the meat, and the cheese in separate containers and place in center of table.

4. Pour broth into 4 soup bowls and let each person build his or her soup with all the things on the table.

5. Garnish each bowl of soup with parsley and Parmesan cheese. You may even top with some of your homemade croutons (page 58).

__What You Get:__ A "fun soup" that serves 4 people!

One-Step / One-Pot Harvest Stew

M-m-m! I love those vegies!

What You Need:

- 1 pound stew meat
- 3 carrots
- 3 potatoes
- 2 stalks celery
- 1 onion
- ½ green pepper
- 1 cup zucchini or yellow crook-neck squash
- 1 slice bread (broken in small pieces)
- 3 Tablespoons tapioca
- 1 bay leaf
- 1 cup stewed tomatoes
- 1 cup water
- 2 teaspoons salt
- large pot with cover

What You Do:

1. In large pot place stew meat.
2. Cut all the vegetables into small chunks and add to meat.
3. Stir in bread, tapioca, bay leaf, tomatoes, water, and salt.
4. Cover pot and bake at 325° for 3½ hours.

What You Get:

A steaming stew for a crisp fall evening or cold winter night that's full of garden vegies!

Melissa's Sleepyhead Instant Breakfast

What You Need:

1 banana
½ cup orange juice
½ cup milk
1 teaspoon honey
1 teaspoon wheat germ
1 egg
blender

What You Do:

1. Put all ingredients into blender.

2. Blend for 1 minute.

3. Pour into tall glass and enjoy!

What You Get:

Quick energy before school!

Celebration Foods for Holidays and Special Days

Make-Ahead Special Breakfast Souffle

...just perfect for Mother's Day
Father's Day
Easter morning
or
anytime!

What You Need:

6-8 slices bread
2 cups grated cheese
     (½ pound)
4 eggs
2 cups milk
1 teaspoon dry mustard
½ teaspoon salt
a sprinkle of pepper

7½ x 12 inch pan

...or try it some day
when you want to give
Mom or Dad a morning
off from the kitchen!

What You Do:

and you do all this the night before!

1. Spread 1 cup of cheese over bottom of baking dish.
2. Cover cheese with bread slices so they just fit.
3. Sprinkle rest of cheese over bread.
4. Beat eggs. Add milk, mustard, salt, and pepper. Mix and pour over bread.
5. Cover and refrigerate all night.
6. In the morning take off cover and bake 45 minutes at 325°.

What You Get:

A puffy golden treat
(so serve it right away)!

Tuna Treat Sandwiches

for when your best friend comes to lunch!

What You Need:

1 small can tuna
¼ cup yogurt
nutritious bread

small bowl

What You Do:

1. Mix tuna with yogurt.
2. Spread on bread for sandwiches.
3. Serve with apples and carrot sticks.

What You Get:

A mix that will make about 4 sandwiches!

You can also dress up the tuna spread with a little chopped celery, pickle, or pickle relish!

Grapefruit - Honey Broil

What You Need:

2 grapefruit

honey

raspberry jam
   (or strawberry)

broiler pan

What You Do:

Be sure to watch carefully so it doesn't burn!

1. Cut grapefruit in halves.

2. Spread each grapefruit half with about a Tablespoon of honey, then add a spot of jam in the center.

3. Broil in the oven until golden.

What You Get:

A sweet-sour surprise that will serve 4 at breakfast or anytime!

Popovers

What You Need:

1 cup unbleached flour
½ teaspoon salt
1 cup milk
2 eggs

medium bowl
muffin pan

What You Get:

6 puffy popovers!

Try these "high hat" muffins with the hole in the center!

What You Do:

1. In mixing bowl put all ingredients and beat all at once just until smooth (over beating makes them smaller).

2. Grease muffin tins well and fill each one about 3/4 full.

3. Bake at 425° for 40-45 minutes.

4. Serve immediately while still warm with butter, jam, and honey, or fill with creamed seafood or meat (see next page).

Lynn's Easy Cheesy Cream Sauce

This always adds a special touch!

What You Need:

2 Tablespoons unbleached flour
2 Tablespoons margarine
2 cups milk
½ teaspoon salt
dash of pepper
½ cup cheddar cheese, grated

small saucepan
wire beater, whisk

What You Do:

1. In saucepan melt margarine and stir in flour.

2. Keep stirring with wire whisk and add milk. Stir until thick and smooth.

3. Add salt and pepper.

4. Stir in cheese just until melted.

What You Get:

A smooth sauce to use over hard-boiled eggs, tuna, macaroni, toast, or mix with ham and peas and pour into popovers (page 74)!

75

76

Banana-Nut Birthday Cake

What You Need:

½ cup margarine

1¼ cups sugar

2 eggs

2 bananas, mashed

½ cup buttermilk

½ teaspoon baking powder

¾ teaspoon baking soda

1 teaspoon salt

2¼ cups unbleached flour

½ cup chopped nuts

2 8-inch or 9-inch cake pans

 and here's what you do...

What You Do:

1. Peel and mash ripe bananas.

2. In a bowl combine margarine and sugar and beat. Add eggs, bananas, and buttermilk.

3. Beat with mixer for 2 minutes.

4. Add baking powder, baking soda, salt, and flour.

5. Beat for 2 more minutes.

6. Fold in nuts.

7. Grease and then flour the 2 pans.

8. Pour batter in pans and bake at 350° for 30 minutes.

...and What You Get is:

the perfect cake for a special occasion!

Friendship Frosting

You can add candles♪ and sing "Happy Birthday"!

What You Need:

1 egg white
⅛ teaspoon salt
½ cup honey
½ teaspoon vanilla

½ cup coconut

medium-sized bowl
a helpful friend

What You Get:

Enough frosting for a nine-inch cake!

What You Do:

1. Beat the egg white with salt until peaks form. (Take turns with a friend.)

2. After peaks form, keep beating and have your friend add the honey in a thin stream (very slowly). Add vanilla.

3. Decorate cake with frosting. Sprinkle coconut over top.

Spread frosting thinly between layers, frost top and let it drizzle down the sides.

79

Baked Apples

Did you know that an apple a day keeps the doctor away?

Do this the night before— It will be ready in the morning!

What You Need:

1 apple for each person
raisins, nuts
margarine, water
brown sugar, cinnamon
yogurt
honey

crock pot

What You Get:

Something special to wake up to... How about the first day of school?

What You Do:

1. Core apples - almost to the bottom.

2. Fill each apple with:
   1 teaspoon margarine
   1 teaspoon brown sugar
   dash of cinnamon, raisins, nuts

3. Add 3/4 cup water to crock pot.

4. Place apples in pot, turn on low.

5. In the morning — remove from pot, top with yogurt and honey.

80

Maple-Syrup Snow Ice Cream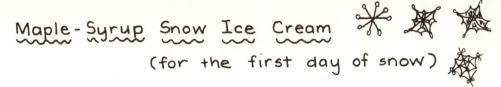
(for the first day of snow)

What You Need:

> a snowy day
> ½ cup milk
> ¾ cup maple syrup
> large pan

♪ Let it snow,
let it snow, let
it snow! ♫

What You Do:

1. Place clean snow in a large pan with milk.
2. Pour maple syrup over snow.
3. Mix and celebrate!

What You Get:

A cool treat and lots of fun!

(inspired by Laura Ingalls Wilder)

Crunchy Oven-Fried Chicken

(for when Grandma comes to visit...)

What You Need:

1 cut-up frying chicken
1 small carton sour cream
2 cups cornflakes
½ teaspoon salt
1 teaspoon onion salt
1½ teaspoons paprika
¼ teaspoon pepper

a plastic bag
large baking pan

What You Do:

1. Rinse chicken and dip each piece in sour cream.

2. Put cornflakes in a plastic bag with spices.

3. Drop in chicken parts two at a time and shake the bag.

4. When well-coated, put into baking dish.

5. Bake at 350° for one hour.

we love you,
♥ Grandma!

Hint: Scrub one baking potato for each person and put into oven next to chicken. Be sure to poke each potato with a fork so it won't explode in the oven!

...or fix a Shamrock Spud (page 90) for a potato with "trimmings"!

What You Get:

A delicious chicken dinner that will bring a smile from Grandma!

Liebert's Log Cabin

Lincoln Log

Happy Birthday, Abe!

What You Need:

2 cups heavy cream, 1 pint
   (for whipping)
3 Tablespoons powdered sugar
½ teaspoon almond extract
32 squares graham crackers

You can even make your own graham crackers (page 46)

   small bowl
   serving platter
   chopped nuts, fruit

What You Get:

A delicious frozen dessert you can decorate with nuts and fruit that will serve 6-8 people!

What You Do:

1. In small bowl beat cream with sugar and almond extract until stiff peaks form.

Now you know how to make whipped cream!

2. Spoon whipped cream on each cracker — stacking 4 at a time.

3. Place groups of 4 crackers and whipped cream together to form one long log.

4. Freeze.

Vegetable - Rice Bake

What You Need:

1½ cups rice
1 teaspoon onion salt
1 package frozen broccoli,
   thawed (or spinach)

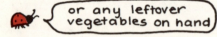
or any leftover vegetables on hand

3 cups milk
2 eggs
1 teaspoon Worcestershire sauce
1 cup cheddar cheese, grated
4 Tablespoons butter

baking dish 8 x 12

What You Do:

1. Mix first 6 ingredients together in 8 x 12 inch baking pan.

2. Put cheese on top of rice mixture and dot with butter.

3. Cover and bake at 350° for 1 hour.

What You Get:

A thrifty main dish for 6 people!

serve a tossed salad with this dish and your meal is complete!

Marvelous Meat Loaf

An energy-saving tip! — Bake some Shamrock Spuds (page 90) along with your loaf and let your oven do double duty!

What You Need:

1 cup bread cubes
2 Tablespoons wheat germ
⅓ cup minced onions
1 Tablespoon minced green pepper
1 egg, slightly beaten
1 pound lean ground beef with
        soy extender
1 Tablespoon horseradish
1¼ teaspoons salt
½ teaspoon dry mustard
2 Tablespoons milk
2 Tablespoons Ketchup
        and
¼ cup Ketchup

large bowl
shallow baking pan

What You Do:

1. Cube bread and chop finely the onions and green pepper.

2. In large bowl, beat egg slightly with a fork.

3. Gently mix in meat, then bread cubes, wheat germ, onions, and pepper.

4. Add horseradish, salt, mustard, milk, 2 Tablespoons Ketchup. Combine lightly but well.

5. Shape meat into loaf and put in shallow baking pan. Spread top with ¼ cup Ketchup.

6. Bake 50-60 minutes at 350°.

This hearty loaf will make any day special!

What You Get: A tasty dish that serves 4-5 people!

87

Frosty Valentine Cupcakes

What You Need:

1 cup plain yogurt
¼ cup powdered sugar
1 16-ounce can whole cranberry
           sauce
1 8-ounce can crushed
    pineapple (with natural juices)

12-cup muffin pan
cupcake papers

I Love • You • I Love • You

What You Do:

Be mine!

1. In medium bowl mix together yogurt and sugar.

2. Add cranberry sauce and crushed pineapple. Stir.

3. Pour mixture into paper liners that have been set into muffin pan.

4. Place pan with mix in freezer until it is frozen.

5. Remove cupcakes from freezer about 5 minutes before eating.

A deliciously delicate valentine's treat!

What You Get:

One dozen frozen cupcakes!

Shamrock Spuds

Happy St. Patrick's Day!

What You Need:

4 baking potatoes
4 Tablespoons margarine
1 cup cheddar cheese, grated
fresh parsley, chopped

The parsley adds a touch of green for St. Patrick's Day!

What You Get:

4 steaming potatoes dressed with cheese and parsley — great to serve with meat loaf (page 87) or Crunchy Oven-Fried Chicken (page 82)!

What You Do:

1. Scrub potatoes well.

2. Pierce with a fork so they don't burst while baking).

3. Bake at 375° for 1 hour.

4. Carefully remove from oven with potholders.

5. Make a slice across each potato, squeeze open and put in each one a Tablespoon of margarine. Sprinkle with grated cheese and chopped parsley.

Windy Weather Chili

What You Need:

- 2 Tablespoons vegetable oil
- 1 medium onion, chopped
- 2 Tablespoons chopped green pepper
- ½ pound lean ground beef with soy extender
- ⅔ cup hot water
- 1 cup canned tomatoes
- 1½ Tablespoons chili powder
- ¼ teaspoon salt
- 1 minced garlic
- 1 teaspoon sugar
- 2 cups kidney beans, canned

large skillet with cover
(or electric frypan)

What You Do:

1. In skillet heat oil, then cook onions and green pepper until tender.

2. Add meat and cook until brown.

3. Add rest of ingredients except beans. Cover pan and let simmer for 1 hour.

4. Uncover and let simmer another ½ hour. (You may add a little more water if mixture becomes too thick.)

5. Just before serving add beans and heat.

I like it best with a scoop of cottage cheese on top!

What You Get:

A hearty hot dish to come in to after a day of kite-flying! (Will serve 4-6 people.)

92

Easter Bunny Carrot Cake

That bunny is sure a good cook! Yum!

What You Need:

2/3 cup vegetable oil
1 1/3 cups sugar
2 cups unbleached flour
1/2 cup whole wheat flour
1 1/4 teaspoons baking soda
1 1/4 teaspoons baking powder
1 teaspoon salt
1 teaspoon cinnamon
1/2 teaspoon nutmeg
1 cup plain yogurt
2 1/2 cups grated carrots
1/2 cup chopped walnuts

large bowl
bundt pan

What You Do:

1. In large bowl mix all ingredients in order given.

2. Grease bundt pan.

3. Bake at 350° for 55 minutes (or until toothpick inserted in center comes out clean).

4. Cool in pan for 15 minutes before removing.

What You Get:

A rich, moist cake - enough to delight 10-12 Easter egg hunters!

Fresh Fruit Torte

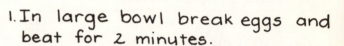

For celebrating the end of school and the beginning of summer vacation!

What You Need:

Sponge Cake —

3 eggs
3/4 cup sugar
1/3 cup hot water
1 teaspoon vanilla
1 1/4 cups unbleached flour
1 teaspoon baking powder
1/2 teaspoon salt

baking pan 9"x 9"

and raspberries or
strawberries
and 1 pint whipping cream

large bowl

What You Do:

1. In large bowl break eggs and beat for 2 minutes.

2. Slowly add sugar, hot water, and vanilla. Continue beating.

3. Quickly add flour, baking powder, and salt. Mix.

4. Grease baking pan and sprinkle flour over pan.

5. Pour batter into pan. Bake at 325° for 25 minutes.

6. When cool, cut into serving portions and serve on individual dishes. Add freshly washed berries. Top with whipped cream. (see page 85.)

What You Get:

6-8 servings of cake!

July Ice Cream Pie

What You Need:

½ cup peanut butter
½ cup corn syrup
2½ cups Special K
  or crispy rice cereal
1 quart ice cream,
        softened

~

saucepan
9" pie plate

What You Get:

A delicious and crunchy treat for 6-8 people on this celebration day!

What You Do:

1. In saucepan heat peanut butter and corn syrup on low heat just until blended.

2. Add cereal and mix thoroughly.

3. Put into pie plate, firmly pressing cereal to bottom and sides of plate. Freeze for 20 minutes.

4. Add ice cream which has been softened enough to gently swirl.

5. Cover with plastic wrap and return to freezer.

6. Remove 10 minutes before serving!

96

Witches' Cauldron Hot Spiced Apple Brew

What You Need:

2 quarts apple juice
   (unfiltered if possible)
1/3 cup brown sugar
3 cinnamon sticks
fresh orange slices
   (cut in half)
5 whole cloves

large saucepan

Stirring and stirring and stirring my brew...

What You Do:

1. Mix apple juice with sugar in large pan.

2. Slice oranges, cut in half, add cloves and cinnamon sticks.

3. Bring to boil.

4. Cover pan. Set stove on "simmer" for 30 minutes.

What You Get:

A spooky brew that serves 8-10 trick-or-treaters!

Kurt's Cookie Monsters

What You Need:

¾ cup shortening
½ cup white sugar
¼ cup brown sugar
1 cup molasses
4 cups unbleached flour
1 teaspoon baking soda
½ teaspoon salt

1½ teaspoons ginger
¾ teaspoon cloves
¼ cup water
½ teaspoon nutmeg
¼ teaspoon allspice
1 Tablespoon rum extract
nuts, raisins, coconut

large bowl
cookie sheet

Find out what you do
...on the next page...

What You Do:

1. In large bowl beat shortening and sugar together until creamy.

2. Add molasses and rum extract and mix.

3. Add flour and spices and water. Beat well.

4. Wrap dough in foil and chill 3-4 hours or overnight.

5. Roll dough about ¼ inch thick. Cut with a 4-inch metal can or cookie cutter. Make monster faces with raisins and nuts and use coconut for hair.

6. Bake at 375° for 8-10 minutes.

What You Get:

About 2 dozen cookies with scary faces!

Pilgrims' Pumpkin Bread

What You Need:

2½ cups unbleached flour
1 cup whole wheat flour
4 eggs
2 cups sugar
⅔ cup vegetable oil
⅔ cup water
⅓ cup wheat germ
2 teaspoons baking soda
1½ teaspoons salt
1 teaspoon cloves
1 teaspoon cinnamon
1 teaspoon nutmeg
2 cups pumpkin
1 cup raisins

a large bowl
2 loaf pans

What You Do:

1. In a large bowl place all the ingredients and beat together until well blended.
2. Stir in raisins.
3. Grease 2 loaf pans and divide up the batter between them.
4. Bake at 325° for about 1 hour (or until done).
5. Remove from pans and let cool.
6. Put cooled loaves in plastic bags and store in refrigerator.
7. Slice thinly to serve.

Yum! Yum! I'm thankful for pumpkin bread!

What You Get:

2 yummy loaves for Thanksgiving dinner!

Christmas Candle Fruit Salad

What You Need:

1 banana
2 pineapple rings
2 cherries (or berries)
2 lettuce leaves

What You Get:

2 Christmas decorations that you can <u>eat</u>!

What You Do:

1. Peel banana, cut in half crosswise.
2. Place pineapple rings on lettuce leaves and stand banana halves up inside the rings.
3. Place a cherry or other red berry on tip of each banana.

Christmas Cranberry Punch

What You Need:

1 quart cranberry juice cocktail
1 quart unsweetened pineapple juice
1 cup orange juice
1 cup water
⅓ cup brown sugar
1 lemon, sliced
12 cloves
2 cinnamon sticks

large kettle, pot

Silent Night...

What You Do:

1. In large pot put juices and water.

2. Stick cloves into lemon slices and add to liquids along with sugar and cinnamon sticks.

3. Simmer for 10 minutes. Serve hot!

What You Get:

14 cups of sparkly punch!

Serve some to the carolers!

Gingerbread Modeling Dough

What You Need:

1/4 cup margarine
1/2 cup brown sugar
1/2 cup molasses
3 1/2 cups unbleached flour
1 teaspoon soda
1/4 teaspoon cloves
1/2 teaspoon cinnamon
1 teaspoon ginger
1/2 teaspoon salt
1/3 cup water

large bowl
cookie sheet

for a spicy Christmas treat!

What You Do:

1. In large bowl mix well the margarine and the sugar.

2. Beat in the molasses.

3. Add the flour, soda, cloves, cinnamon, ginger, and salt.

4. Add the water and mix well, using your hands to mix the flour in when the dough becomes stiff.

5. Now the dough is ready to model into gingerbread boys or girls or anything you wish.

6. Place modeled dough on greased cookie sheet. Bake the dough at 350° for 8-10 minutes or longer, depending on its thickness.

<u>What You Get:</u>

About eight, 5-inch-long fat gingerbread boys and girls, or 16 thinner ones — plus a lot of fun too!

Vegetable Christmas Tree Centerpiece

What You Need:

1 styrofoam cone tree
toothpicks
cherry tomatoes
cauliflower "flowerets"
sliced cucumbers
black olives
broccoli
cheese cubes...
            etc.

What You Do:

1. Spear each vegetable and cheese with a toothpick.

2. "Decorate" your Christmas tree with speared goodies.

3. Serve sour cream dip on the side (see next page).

"nibble nibble"

Snowy Sour Cream Dip

and here's

 ## What You Need:

> 1 cup sour cream
>   (or yogurt)
> 2 Tablespoons chopped parsley
> 1/8 teaspoon curry powder
> 1/2 teaspoon salt
> 1/4 teaspoon paprika
> 2 Tablespoons chopped
>   green onions

What You Get:

An "incredible edible" that's
nice too for decoration—
as well as eating!

What You Do:

1. Chop parsley and onion.

2. Mix together all the
   ingredients.

3. Chill in refrigerator for
   one hour.

4. If you like you may
   add a small amount of
   shellfish- clam, shrimp,
   or crab.

New Year's Eve Popcorn Party

Happy New Year, everyone!

What You Need:

6-8 cups popped corn
1/3 cup melted margarine
1/4 cup Parmesan cheese
dash of salt to taste

large bowl
lots of napkins

and good friends, of course!

What You Do:

1. In large bowl stir together popcorn, melted margarine, Parmesan cheese, and salt.

2. Now pass the popcorn around and enjoy sharing your "New Year's Resolutions" with one another! Talk about the old year and welcome in the new!

What You Get:

A treat that serves many and makes for good munching and pleasant memories!

"Make new friends and keep the old, one is silver, and the other's gold!"

Picnic, Camping, and Outdoor Foods

Marcia's Gold Mine Sandwich

What You Need:

a slice of your favorite bread
margarine
1 egg
salt and pepper to taste
grated cheese, cheddar, jack,
    or swiss

griddle or fry pan
round cookie cutter

What You Do:

1. Preheat frying pan over medium heat.

2. Butter a slice of bread on both sides and then cut a hole in the middle of it with your cutter.

You can nibble on the little piece while you are waiting!

3. Toast the buttered bread on both sides in the pan turning it with a spatula.

4. When the bread is a nice golden color, <u>carefully</u> break open the egg and pour it into the hole of the bread.

5. Sprinkle the egg with salt and pepper and scatter the grated cheese over the whole thing.

6. Cover the pan so that the egg becomes firm (or just the way you like it) and the cheese is melted.

7. Lift the "sandwich" out of the pan with the spatula and put it on a plate.

<u>What You Get</u>:

A yummy egg and toast that is fun to eat for breakfast, lunch, or anytime!

"Triple B" Burgers

What You Need:

2 Tablespoons vegetable oil
1½ pounds lean ground beef
  and soy extender
¼ cup chopped onions
1 cup chopped celery
1 teaspoon salt
1 teaspoon dry mustard
1 teaspoon vinegar
1 teaspoon Worcestershire sauce
¾ cup ketchup
1 Tablespoon horseradish
¾ cup water
6 buns

large skillet, frying pan

... for all you cowpokes—
this brand stands for
"Barbecue Burgers on
        a Bun"!

→

What You Do:

1. In large skillet brown meat and onions in vegetable oil.
2. Add the rest of the ingredients and simmer for one hour. Stir every once in awhile.
3. Spoon into warm or toasted bun and serve immediately.

What You Get:
6 hearty sandwiches - a real western treat for cowboys and cowgirls!

What can you do with a shish kebab?

It's a meal on a stick!

Fruit Sticks

What You Need:

12 chunks banana
12 chunks pineapple
12 strawberries
12 orange sections
coconut, grated

4 skewers

What You Do:

1. Alternate fruit on skewers and roll in coconut.

2. Put on barbecue grill.

3. Turn after 3 minutes. Cook for 3 more minutes.

Vegetable Sticks

What You Need:

12 cherry tomatoes
1 green pepper, sliced
12 mushrooms

4 skewers

What You Do:

1. Alternate vegetables on skewers.

2. Grill as above.

Meat Sticks

What You Need:

12 small chunks ham
12 chunks pineapple
12 chunks green pepper
12 mushrooms

4 skewers

What You Do:

1. Alternate meat and vegetables.

2. Grill as above.

✱ What You Get:

4 shish kebabs! Great to eat!

1-2-3 Skillet

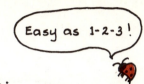

Easy as 1-2-3!

What You Need:

1 pound ground beef
   with soy extender
1½ cups brown rice
3 cups water
¼ cup soy sauce
2 teaspoons salt
dash pepper

skillet, with lid
campfire, grill

What You Do:

1. In large skillet brown meat.

2. Add rice, water, soy sauce, salt, and a dash of pepper.

3. Cover tightly and cook for 40 minutes, or until done.

What You Get:

A meal in a skillet for 4 campers!

Roasted Apple on a Stick

An around-the-campfire snack...

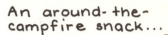

What You Need:

apples (small)
honey or melted margarine
cinnamon and sugar mix

long sticks of green wood
a good campfire

What You Get:

A baked apple on a stick!

Be careful not to burn your tongue!

What You Do:

1. Spear a small apple (or cut a larger one into halves) with a long stick.

2. Hold the apple over warm coals (not too hot) and turn it until it becomes soft and ready to eat.

3. When it is cool enough to take a bite, the apple may be dipped in honey or melted margarine and a mixture of cinnamon and sugar.

Pocket Stew

This is sure to be a favorite!

What You Need:

1¼ pounds lean ground beef
with soy extender
2 potatoes
2 carrots
1 small onion
salt and pepper
parsley
1 Tablespoon Worcestershire
sauce

aluminum foil
campfire

What You Do:

1. Divide meat into 4 pieces. Set each piece on aluminum foil and press to make 4 very flat patties.

2. Slice thin or grate unpeeled vegetables (potatoes, carrots, and onions, or any others you might wish) into bowls.

3. Place some of each chopped vegetable on meat patty. Sprinkle with salt, pepper, parsley, and Worcestershire sauce.

4. Fold the patty over so that it is half the size, forming a pocket with the vegetables inside. Seal the edges.

5. Wrap meat tightly in the heavy aluminum foil.

6. Place foil packets over grill or campfire and cook. The vegetables will steam inside the meat.

7. Cook about 45 minutes.

What You Get:

4 hearty pockets to satisfy hungry hikers.

Strawberry Leather

What You Need:

1 quart strawberries

blender
large shallow pan

What You Get:

A tasty strawberry treat!

What You Do:

1. Place 2 cups of the strawberries into blender. Blend for 1 minute or until smooth.

2. Blend remaining berries and then pour all berries into pan.

3. Cover with cheesecloth. Tape the cloth to the pan.

4. Place pan outside for 2 hot days (bring inside at night).

5. When berries are dry and "leathery," roll up.

Camp Cobbler

It's berry picking time

What You Need:

2 cups wild berries
(huckleberries,
blueberries, or
blackberries)
¼ cup honey
1 cup coconut
3 Tablespoons brown sugar
½ cup unbleached flour
½ cup wheat germ or
oatmeal
¼ teaspoon salt
3 Tablespoons margarine

cooking pan, tinfoil
bowl

What You Do:

1. Gather berries in the woods, place in pan, drizzle with honey.

2. In another bowl mix everything together except margarine. Pat mixture evenly over berries. Dot with margarine.

3. Cook on rack over low coals, cover top with tinfoil.

What You Get: A campfire dessert!

Susie's Wrap-Arounds

What You Need:

> large lettuce leaves
> thin slices of ham, or
>   beef and cheese
> salad dressing
> bean sprouts or
>   alfalfa sprouts
> toothpicks

> I love picnics-
> don't you?

What You Do:

1. Lay out lettuce leaf on flat surface.

2. Top with meat and cheese, add a small amount of salad dressing.

3. Sprinkle sprouts over all, roll up and secure with a toothpick.

What You Get:

An easy-to-make, easy-to-eat picnic treat!

Banana S'mores

You'll always want s'more!

What You Need:

2 bananas
graham crackers
marshmallows

~

skewer or
long stick

What You Get:

Several s'mores
with a difference!

What You Do:

1. Spear marshmallows with a stick or skewer and toast over fire to a golden brown.

2. Place marshmallow on one graham cracker square and add sliced bananas.

3. Top with another graham cracker.

4. Eat and enjoy!

And for a change, try making them with peanut butter in place of marshmallow.

# Grilled Corn-on-the-Cob

Be sure to try this on your next picnic or camping trip!

What You Need:

> fresh ears of corn
>   (in the husks)
> butter or margarine
> salt
>
>   campfire, grill

What You Get:

Tender and delicious corn – ready to eat right on the cob!

What You Do:

1. Pull husk down on each ear of corn and carefully remove the "hair" (cornsilk).
2. Pull husk back up and soak ears in cold water for 15-30 minutes.
3. Place ears (in husks) on grill and cook 15-20 minutes.
4. When the inside steams and the outer husk is dry and turning brown, the corn is done.
5. Remove husks to serve. Spread with butter and salt to enjoy this outdoor treat.

Try this with Fresh Fried Fish (page 126).

124

Hobo Special

What You Need:

> 1 pound stew meat
> 6 carrots
> 3 potatoes
> 1 10-ounce package frozen peas
> 1 8-ounce can corn
> 3 cups water or bouillon
> salt and pepper
>
> 4-6 empty soup cans
> aluminum foil
> campfire, grill

What You Get:

Dinner in a can for 4-6 hungry hobos!

What You Do:

1. Cut up stew meat in small bite-sized pieces. Slice the carrots and potatoes thin and mix together with remaining ingredients (except bouillon).

2. Wash cans and fill with meat and vegetables.

3. Add ½ cup bouillon to each can.

4. Cover can with aluminum foil and punch holes in top.

5. Place cans on grill over low fire and cook about one hour or one hour and 15 minutes.

Be careful handling the hot cans!

Fresh Fried Fish

First you catch a fish... good luck!

What You Need:

freshly caught fish
1/2 cup cornmeal
dash salt and pepper
2 Tablespoons margarine

campfire
frying pan

What You Get:

A successful "fish story"!

What You Do:

1. Clean the fish! Get some help with this.

2. Dip the washed fish in cornmeal seasoned with salt and pepper.

3. Place frying pan on grill.

4. Melt margarine in pan and add fish.

5. Fry about 4-6 minutes on each side until tender.

What can you put in a pocket?

Fill pita pocket bread
with any of the following:

1. Peanut butter and honey, jelly or jam.

2. Alfalfa sprouts, chopped tomatoes,
cucumber, avocado with bits of ham,
bacon or leftover meat and a teaspoon
of mayonnaise.

3. Tuna fish salad (see page 72)

4. Egg salad
Chop 2 hard-boiled eggs. Add a
Tablespoon of mayonnaise. Add salt
and pepper to taste, 1/4 teaspoon dry
mustard, and chopped parsley or pickles.
...and lots more!

what can you think of to put in a pocket?

Delicious Dumplings

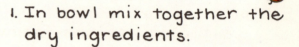

A tasty and filling addition to any soup or stew you have simmering over the fire!

What You Need:

- 2 cups unbleached flour
- 3 teaspoons baking powder
- 1 teaspoon salt
- 1 Tablespoon instant minced onions
- 1 Tablespoon dried parsley
- ½ teaspoon sage (if you like)
- ½ cup powdered dry milk
- ⅓ cup shortening or margarine
- 1 cup water
- mixing bowl

The mix may be made ahead of time and water added at campsite.

What You Get:

Enough dumplings to feed 4-5 hungry campers!

What You Do:

1. In bowl mix together the dry ingredients.

2. Add shortening. With 2 knives, cut in shortening until mixture is coarse.

3. With fork, lightly mix in water to form soft dough. (Stir as little as possible.)

4. Drop dough by tablespoonfuls in boiling stew or soup.

5. Simmer dumplings 10 minutes uncovered; then cover and simmer 5-10 minutes more.

Camp Sweyolaken Orange Muffins

Baked right in a fresh orange skin!

What You Need:

6 oranges
your favorite muffin batter

> I suggest the muffin recipe on the package of Krusteaz Whole Wheat 'n Honey Pancake Mix or Make-Ahead Muffin Mix on page 62.

aluminum foil
campfire, grill

What You Get:

Six marvelous muffins with the flavor of fresh oranges!

What You Do:

1. Cut off tops of oranges. Scoop out orange sections with a spoon and eat!

> Good vitamin C!

2. Make your favorite muffin mix.

3. Fill each orange ⅔ full with muffin batter.

4. Wrap each orange tightly with aluminum foil.

5. Bake on campfire or grill for 30-35 minutes.

Slumber Party Pizzas

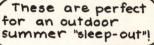

These are perfect for an outdoor summer "sleep-out"!

What You Need:

6 English muffins
1 pound lean ground beef
1 small can tomato sauce
cheddar cheese, grated
salt, pepper, oregano

extras:
   olives
   mushrooms
   fresh tomatoes
    etc.

What You Do:

1. Split the muffins and spread each half with tomato sauce.

2. Crumble ground beef over sauce, sprinkle with salt, pepper, and oregano (just a dab!)

3. Put on broiler pan and place under broiler until meat is brown.

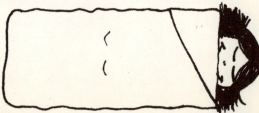

4. Remove from oven (use oven mitts) and sprinkle cheese on top. Place under broiler again until cheese melts.

5. The "extras" you choose may be sprinkled over the cheese and heated while the cheese melts.

6. Keep oven door open while broiling so you can see what's going on — it's fun to peek!

What You Get:

Enough mini-pizzas to fill 6 empty tummies and give you enough energy to talk until midnight!

A Spreadable Edible

(for sandwiches)

What You Need:

½ cup peanut butter
½ cup cream cheese
1 Tablespoon honey
⅓ cup dates, chopped
(or raisins)

medium bowl

What You Do:

1. In bowl mix peanut butter and cream cheese together.

2. Add honey and raisins or dates.

3. Keep your spread in a covered jar in the refrigerator. It's ready to use anytime!

What You Get:

A terrific topping for your favorite bread — whole wheat, raisin, oatmeal, or banana bread!

Or try it on celery! Yum!

Foods from Other Lands

Hawaiian Surprise-Top Pie

Hooray for the 50th state!

What You Need:

4 eggs
2 cups milk
6 Tablespoons margarine
½ cup unbleached flour
½ cup sugar
1 teaspoon almond or
     vanilla extract
1 cup grated coconut
     blender
10" pie pan

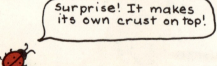

Surprise! It makes its own crust on top!

What You Do:

1. Mix everything but coconut into blender.

2. Add coconut. Blend for 5 seconds. (Count 1-2-3-4-5.)

3. Pour mixture into greased and floured pie pan.

4. Bake at 350° for 50-60 minutes.

What You Get:

A tropical treat of a pie with a crusty coconut top!

Golden Eggs
from France

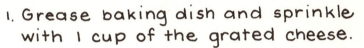
Oui! Oui! I love the way the French do these eggs!

What You Need:

6 eggs
2 cups grated cheese
   (swiss or cheddar)
¼ cup cream or
   evaporated milk
salt and pepper to taste
chopped parsley
dash of paprika

shallow pan
8" x 12"

What You Get:

A deliciously easy breakfast dish that will serve 6!

What You Do:

1. Grease baking dish and sprinkle with 1 cup of the grated cheese.

2. Make 6 wells or holes in the cheese with a spoon.

3. Carefully break an egg into each hole.

4. Sprinkle the cream over the top, then the salt, pepper, parsley, and paprika.

5. Spread rest of cheese over all. Bake at 375° for 25 minutes.

135

Ghana Coconut Chips

What You Need:

1 fresh coconut

large corkscrew
potato peeler
hammer
cookie sheet
an adult or
   older friend to help

What You Do:

1. With corkscrew open 3 holes at the end of the coconut — right in the monkey face. ☺

2. Drain milk — it's good to drink!

3. Bake coconut on cookie sheet in 200° oven until it cracks, 30-40 minutes.

4. Now crack open the coconut — ask an adult or older friend to use a hammer.

5. Crack off outer shell and thin brown shell. Then use a potato peeler to slice off thin chips of coconut onto a cookie sheet.

6. Bake at 200° for 2 hours. Remove from oven and stir thoroughly — now return to oven and bake at 150° for 2-4 more hours.

What You Get:

An unusually delicious, nutritious snack! Some people like to sprinkle salt on them — try it!

store in tight jar!

Swedish Cabbage 'n Apple Salad

What You Need:

1 small cabbage
2 apples
2 Tablespoons orange juice
½ cup heavy cream or
    mayonnaise
1 Tablespoon sugar

grater
large bowl
small bowl

What You Do:

1. Shred cabbage on coarse grater into large bowl.

2. Wash and chop unpeeled apples and stir together with cabbage.

3. In small bowl mix together the cream (or mayonnaise), orange juice, and sugar.

4. Pour mixture over cabbage and apples. Stir.

5. Chill in refrigerator until ready to serve.

What You Get:

A crisp salad that serves 4 for lunch — or 6 helpings along with dinner.

138

Canadian Eggnog

What You Need:

3 eggs
¼ cup honey
3 cups cold milk
dash salt
nutmeg

～

blender

What You Do:

1. Put all the ingredients in a blender except the nutmeg and mix for 30 seconds.

2. Pour into glasses and sprinkle nutmeg on top.

What You Get:

3-4 frothy glasses of eggnog!

Fondue Fun
from Switzerland

What You Need:

2 cups chunky peanut butter
1 can (5⅓ ounces) evaporated milk
½ cup light brown sugar
½ cube margarine
                and...
cut up apples, bananas, pears
broken graham crackers
bowl of toasted wheat germ
        mixed with coconut

Salton Hot Tray
fondue pot or small pan
fondue forks
friends!

What You Do:

1. Mix peanut butter, milk, sugar, and margarine over low heat until well blended and hot.

2. Carefully place pot on hot tray.

3. Spear fruit on forks, dip in fondue, then dip in coconut wheat germ mix. Graham crackers may be dipped too or eaten plain.

What You Get: A feast for friends and family!

Shelly's Super Simple Spaghetti

What You Need:

1 pound lean ground beef
    and soy extender
1 small onion, chopped
1 small green pepper, chopped
1 small can sliced ripe olives
1 small can mushrooms, drained
1 8-ounce can tomato sauce (1 cup)
2½ cups canned tomatoes
2 cups water
2 teaspoons salt
¼ teaspoon pepper
1 teaspoon Worcestershire sauce
a few drops Tabasco or hot
    sauce (if you like)
4 ounces spaghetti noodles
    (about a fistful)

large skillet, fry pan

Sooo super and sooo simple!

What You Do:

1. In large skillet brown beef; add onions and green pepper. Cook 5 minutes.

2. Add olives, mushrooms, and tomato sauce and mix gently.

3. Add tomatoes, water, salt, pepper, Tabasco, Worcestershire sauce. Stir into meat mixture.

4. Add uncooked spaghetti; stir and let come to a boil.

5. Cover pan tightly, turn down heat to low and let simmer for 40 minutes. Stir every once in awhile.

6. Uncover pan and let mixture simmer for 15 more minutes.

7. Serve and enjoy! Try sprinkling Parmesan cheese over the top of each portion.

<u>What You Get:</u>

A main dish for about 6 people. Everyone loves spaghetti and there won't be lots of pots to wash!

Hooray! Only one pot to wash!

Dutch Puff

What You Need:

1 cup unbleached flour
1 cup milk
4 eggs
⅓ cup margarine

blender
large skillet
or
shallow pan
honey, syrup, or fruit
for topping

It's a puffy pancake--perfect for a special breakfast surprise!

What You Do:

1. Preheat oven to 425.°

2. Place margarine in large shallow pan and put it in the oven until it is hot and bubbly.

3. Put flour, milk, and eggs in blender and mix well (or you may beat with a mixer).

4. Remove margarine pan from the oven <u>VERY</u> carefully!! Use pot holders and ask someone to help!

5. Pour batter into pan of hot melted margarine.

6. Bake at 425° for 20-25 minutes until pancake is high and puffed.

7. Serve immediately! Place pan on a hot pad in the center of the table to show off your Dutch Puff!

<u>What You Get:</u>

Lots of "oohs" and "ahhs" when you bring this out from the oven! It will serve 4 people!

Oriental Chicken Salad

This salad is a meal in itself - especially nice on a warm summer evening!

What You Need:

2 cups cooked chicken,
   or turkey, cubed
1 small can water chestnuts,
   sliced
3 stalks celery, sliced
½ cup almonds, slivered or sliced
1 small can pineapple chunks
1 bunch seedless grapes or
   cubed apples
1 cup fresh bean sprouts
1 cup mayonnaise
½ teaspoon curry powder
½ teaspoon salt
2 teaspoons soy sauce
1 small can mandarin oranges

large bowl

What You Do:

1. In large bowl mix the mayonnaise, soy sauce, curry powder, and salt together.

2. Add all the rest of the ingredients except the mandarin oranges.

3. Chill salad in refrigerator.

4. At serving time decorate with mandarin oranges.

What You Get:

A refreshing salad for 8 people!

Scottish Potato Crisps

What You Need:

2 large potatoes
1 Tablespoon margarine
salt
garlic salt

~

baking sheet
small saucepan

What You Get:

A good potato
snack - a nice
change from
potato chips!

What You Do:

1. Scrub but don't peel potatoes.

2. Slice potatoes <u>very thin</u> - ask for help on this part.

3. Arrange slices on greased baking sheet and bake at 375°.

4. When they are slightly brown use potholders to remove sheet from oven. Turn over potatoes with a spatula to brown other side.

5. In saucepan melt margarine. Pour over potatoes in a bowl and sprinkle with salts.

Bavarian Breakfast Muesli

What You Need:

rolled oats
walnuts
2 bananas
2 apples
2 Tablespoons lemon juice
4 Tablespoons milk
brown sugar
saucepan

What You Get:

A good hearty breakfast for 4 people!

What You Do:

1. Cook rolled oats according to directions on package. (4 servings)

2. While oats are cooking, wash and chop apples.

3. Add apples, lemon juice, and milk to oats. Stir.

4. Decorate with nuts and banana slices (or any fruit you like).

5. If you wish you may sprinkle brown sugar on top.

English Toad in the Hole

What You Need:

1 pound sausages
1 Tablespoon vegetable oil
1 egg
1 cup unbleached flour
1 cup milk
¼ teaspoon salt

mixing bowl
skillet, fry pan
(that can go in oven)

What You Do:

1. In mixing bowl beat together flour, salt, egg, and milk and let stand for 20 minutes.

2. In skillet fry sausages in oil for 5 minutes on each side.

3. Pour batter over sausage.

4. Place skillet in oven and bake at 400° for 30 minutes.

What You Get:

A delicious breakfast or supper treat that serves 5-6 people!

Chinese Fried Rice

It's fun to serve fortune cookies for dessert with this dish!

What You Need:

3 Tablespoons vegetable oil
6 green onions, thinly sliced
1 cup chopped cooked meat
   ham, beef, *Use your leftovers!* or pork

2 eggs, beaten
2 Tablespoons soy sauce
½ teaspoon sugar
 salt and pepper, if needed
4 cups cooked brown or
      white rice, cold

large skillet

What You Get:

Rice for 6 people and a delicious way to use up bits and pieces!

What You Do:

1. Use rice that is leftover or make several hours ahead (page 168).

2. In skillet heat oil over medium heat. Stir in onion and cook for 2 minutes. Add meat and heat.

3. Stir in rice. Coat with oil and meat mixture, frying for 2-3 minutes.

4. Pour beaten eggs over rice. Cook, stirring often until egg is set.

5. Mix soy sauce and sugar, add to rice and stir.

Viennese Beggarman Pudding

This is a delicious way to use up leftover bread!

What You Need:

2 eggs
4 slices stale dry bread (any kind)
1/3 cup raisins
1/4 cup almonds
2 cups applesauce

mixing bowl
square pan
9" x 9"

What You Do:

1. Soak raisins in water to "plump" them while you grate the bread. (You can grate with a hand grater or in a blender.)

2. In a bowl mix applesauce, bread crumbs, and drained raisins.

3. Add chopped almonds and eggs. Beat well.

4. Pour mixture into greased pan and bake at 375° for 30 minutes.

What You Get:

A hearty dessert pudding for 6-8 people. It's delicious when served with a little cream - or maybe you'd like a dab of brown sugar on top!

Brazilian Feijoada
(rice and beans)

What You Need:

1 large onion, chopped
1 clove garlic, minced or powdered
2 Tablespoons vegetable oil
1 cup black beans (or small red)
3½ cups water
1 bay leaf
½ teaspoon cilantro *...if you have it*
   (coriander leaf)
¼ teaspoon pepper
¼ pound ham bits, smoked
   meat, or sausage (if you like)
1 orange half
2 stalks celery, chopped
1 tomato, chopped or
   2 Tablespoons tomato paste

strainer
large pot

What You Do:

*1. Start the beans a day ahead so they can soak overnight and then...

2. In large pot heat oil and cook onion and garlic until tender.

3. Add beans, water, and bay leaf. Cover pot and let soak overnight.

4. Next day add to beans the cilantro, pepper, meat, orange half, celery, and chopped tomato. Simmer covered, for 2-3 hours or more until the beans are tender. Add more water if necessary.

5. Serve these beans over rice (page 168).

What You Get:

In Brazil they sprinkle it with Farofa-a crumbly mixture made from mandioca.

A dish to serve 4 brasileiros! To make it authentic sprinkle with toasted bread crumbs. Serve with orange slices.

Scandinavian Layered Salad

Make it a day ahead!

What You Need:

2 cups shredded lettuce
1/3 cup chopped parsley
1/2 cup chopped green pepper
2 stalks celery, thinly sliced
1 package frozen peas, thawed

> You may also add some grated carrot and zucchini or chopped broccoli and cauliflower.

1 cup mayonnaise
1 Tablespoon sugar
dash salt and pepper
1 cup grated cheddar cheese
1/4 cup thinly sliced green onion

large serving bowl
small bowl

What You Do:

1. On cutting board chop vegetables.

2. In large bowl layer the lettuce, parsley, green pepper, celery, and peas.

3. In small bowl mix together the mayonnaise, sugar, salt, and pepper. Spread mixture over top.

4. Sprinkle grated cheese and onion on top.

5. Cover salad and chill overnight (or several hours) before serving.

__What You Get:__ A vegetable salad for 6!

Grandma's German Honey Cookies

This is a favorite for Christmas in Germany!

What You Need:

1 egg
1/3 cup sugar
2/3 cup honey
1/3 cup soft shortening
2 3/4 cups unbleached flour
1 teaspoon soda
1 teaspoon salt
1 teaspoon vanilla

large bowl
cookie sheet
cookie cutters

What You Get:

About 3 dozen puffy honey cookies!

What You Do:

1. In large bowl place all ingredients and mix together.

2. Sprinkle board or table with flour. Roll dough about 1/4 inch thick.

3. Cut shapes with cookie cutters.

4. Bake at 375° for 8-10 minutes.

5. If you like you may frost with your favorite glaze or frosting.

155

German Eier-Kuchen (Egg Pancakes)

What You Need:

4 eggs
1 cup milk
1 cup unbleached flour
pinch of salt

mixing bowl
small frying pan
pat of margarine

What You Get:

4-6 pancakes!
These are also good
rolled up with applesauce
or cottage cheese!

What You Do:

1. In mixing bowl beat the eggs. Add flour, milk, and salt, and beat more.

2. Put a pat of margarine in a small frying pan on medium heat.

3. When butter is melted pour a thin layer of batter to barely cover bottom of pan.

4. Flip over when bubbles form.

5. When golden brown, sprinkle with a little sugar and lemon.

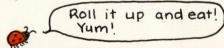

Roll it up and eat! Yum!

Mexican Flying Saucers

What You Need:

> 1 package corn tortillas (12)
> grated cheese
> sliced olives
>
> cookie sheet

What You Do:

1. Sprinkle grated cheese on tortillas.

2. Add olives.

3. Bake in 425° oven for 7 minutes. Remove carefully!

4. Serve warm!

What You Get:

1 package of tortillas makes 12 cheesy treats for snack or even a quick meal!

Olé!

Nifty Nacho Platter

A "south-of-the-border" treat!

What You Need:

1 16-ounce can refried beans
1 pound lean ground beef
    and soy extender
1 small onion, chopped
2 cups grated cheddar cheese
1 4-ounce can roasted green
    chiles (chopped)
¼ cup salsa or taco sauce
toppings (choose what you like):
    4 green onions, chopped
    1 cup sour cream
    1 4-ounce can sliced ripe olives
    1 avocado, mashed
taco shells, broken in quarters

frying pan, skillet
large shallow pan

What You Do:

1. In frying pan brown ground beef and onions.

2. Spread refried beans in center of large baking dish.

3. Sprinkle ground beef and onions over beans, then top with cheese.

4. Spoon chiles over cheese, then pour hot sauce over the top.

5. Bake at 400° for 20 minutes until bean mix is hot and cheese is melted.

6. While the platter is in the oven, prepare whatever toppings you like to go on the mixture.

7. Remove platter from oven. Sprinkle onions and olives over all. Spoon mashed avocado and sour cream in the middle of the mixture.

8. Put the taco shells (broken into dip-sized pieces) all around edge of pan.

9. Place the platter on a hot pad in the center of the table. It's time to dip into the spicy mixture with the taco pieces.

<u>What</u> <u>You</u> <u>Get</u>:
A "dippy dinner" for 4-5 people! It's fun to eat too!

Wendy's Welsh Scones

What You Need:

2 cups unbleached flour
½ cup sugar
1 Tablespoon baking powder
½ teaspoon salt
2 Tablespoons shortening
¾ cup raisins
1 egg
½ cup milk

large bowl
cookie sheet

What You Do:

1. In large bowl mix together all ingredients except the raisins.

2. Add raisins and mix.

3. Grease cookie sheet and drop mix by Tablespoons on sheet.

4. Bake at 350° for 20 minutes.

What You Get:

A dozen scones that melt in your mouth!

Delectable and delicious!

Simple Spanish Gazpacho

What You Need:

1 large can V-8 juice
  (24 ounces)
1 can chicken broth
  (14½ ounces)
juice of ½ lemon
1 Tablespoon vinegar
2 drops Tabasco
salt and pepper to taste
cucumber, finely chopped

blender
serving mugs or bowls

Serve this chilled! It's cool!

What You Do:

1. In blender place all ingredients except cucumber and mix well.

2. Chill mixture in refrigerator.

3. When ready to serve, pour into individual mugs or bowls.

4. Garnish with chopped cucumber.

What You Get:

A super soup for summer that will serve 4-5 people!

> Try this salad with bulgur - it's different and you'll like it!

Tabouli
(A Middle Eastern salad treat)

What You Need:

1 cup bulgur or cracked wheat
2 cups boiling water
2 tomatoes, cut in small pieces
½ cup chopped green onions
1 cup chopped parsley
1 can garbanzo beans, drained
⅓ cup vegetable oil
    (preferably olive oil)
½ cup lemon juice
1 teaspoon salt
dash pepper
lettuce leaves
cheddar cheese sticks
ripe olives

mixing bowl
strainer, sieve

What You Do:

1. In bowl place bulgur. Pour water over it and soak for 1 hour.

2. Use strainer to drain off any extra water, then add tomatoes, onions, parsley, garbanzo beans, oil, lemon juice, salt, and pepper.

3. Mix well, then chill in the refrigerator for at least 2 hours.

4. When ready to serve, spoon on serving plate lined with lettuce leaves. Garnish with cheese sticks and olives.

What You Get: A main dish for 6!

Crunchy Cracked Wheat Pilaf

Another dish from the Middle East!

What You Need:

```
1 cup bulgur or cracked wheat
2 Tablespoons margarine
2 Tablespoons chopped onions
2 Tablespoons chopped celery
2 cups chicken broth or
                    bouillon
1/4 teaspoon oregano
1/2 teaspoon salt

          saucepan
```

What You Get:

A unique dish for 4 people—a little like rice but with a chewy, crunchy texture.

What You Do:

1. In saucepan melt margarine. Stir and cook onion and celery until tender.

2. Add rest of ingredients. Stir.

3. Cover saucepan and turn the heat to high until mixture boils.

4. When mixture begins to boil, lower heat and simmer for 30 minutes.

Danish Open Sandwiches
(Smørebrød)

Beef Sandwich

What You Need:

2 slices rye bread
2 slices beef
1 pickle, sliced
butter
mustard
tomato
parsley

What You Do:

1. Spread bread with butter.
2. Put beef on bread and spread with mustard.
3. Add tomato, pickle, and parsley.

Fish and Egg Sandwich

What You Need:

2 slices rye bread
2 hard-cooked eggs
8 sardines (or anchovies)
butter

What You Do:

1. Spread bread with butter.
2. Put on sardines and sliced eggs.

What You Get: An open-face sandwich for you and 1 friend!

Indian Corn Pudding

What You Need:

3 eggs
2 cups milk
1/4 cup sugar
1 teaspoon salt
1 Tablespoons cornstarch
1 can cream corn
2 Tablespoons margarine
1/4 cup brown sugar

mixing bowl
baking dish (8½" x 12")
larger pan for water

What You Get:

A tasty vegetable side dish to add a special touch to any meal!

What You Do:

1. In bowl beat eggs and milk together.

2. Add sugar, salt, cornstarch, and corn. Stir evenly.

3. Pour into casserole dish which has been placed in a larger pan filled with 1½ inches of hot water.

4. Over top of mixture add dots of margarine and brown sugar.

5. Place pans in oven and bake at 300° for 2½ hours (or until knife inserted in middle comes out clean).

Stir-Fry Chinese Chicken

What You Need:

2 chicken breasts, boned
1 Tablespoon soy sauce
1 Tablespoon cornstarch
1 Tablespoon water
        and
1 green pepper, sliced thin
1-2 cups sliced mushrooms
1 onion, sliced thin

½ cup chicken broth or
        water
1 Tablespoon soy sauce
1 Tablespoon cornstarch
½ teaspoon sugar
5 Tablespoons vegetable oil

small bowl
large bowl
electric fry pan

What You Do:

1. Slice in thin strips the boned chicken.

2. In small bowl mix together soy sauce, water, and cornstarch. Add sliced chicken, stir, and let sit for ½ hour or so while you slice the vegetables.

3. In large bowl mix together chicken broth, soy sauce, cornstarch, and sugar.

4. Slice vegetables very thin and mix into liquid in large bowl.

5. Now you are ready to cook! Set your electric fry pan on medium high and heat 2 Tablespoons of the oil.

6. Pour chicken in its sauce into oil and cook about 5 minutes until it is white and tender. Remove chicken, returning it to the small bowl. Set aside.

7. Add the rest of the oil (3 Tablespoons) and allow to heat.

8. Pour vegetable mixture in its sauce into hot oil and and cook until tender but still crisp. Stir as it cooks (about 5 minutes).

9. Add chicken strips to vegetables. Stir to heat.

10. It's ready to serve with rice or Chinese noodles!

The chopsticks take a little practice!

<u>What</u> <u>You</u> <u>Get</u>:

A chicken dish for 4! Eat with chopsticks for a festive meal!

Basic Brown Rice

What You Need:

> 1 Tablespoon margarine
>   or vegetable oil
> 1 cup brown rice
> ½ teaspoon salt
> 2 cups boiling water
>
> teakettle
> covered saucepan

What You Get:

A fluffy rice that serves 4-6 people and is a wonderful accompaniment to many dishes!

What You Do:

This simple method never fails to make perfect rice every time!

1. In teakettle put at least 2 cups water and put over high heat.

2. While waiting for water to boil place margarine in a saucepan and let it melt. Add rice and salt and stir well.

3. When water boils measure 2 cups and add to rice mixture. Stir well and turn up heat just until water boils again.

4. Cover saucepan, reduce heat and simmer for 40 minutes.

It's done!

Resources: for families who care to know more

Organizations Concerned with World Food Needs:

1. Bread for the World
   6411 Chillum Place, N.W.
   Washington, D.C. 20012

2. CROP
   P.O. Box 968
   Elkhart, Ind. 46514

3. Church World Service
   475 Riverside Drive
   New York, N.Y. 10027

4. Mennonite Central Committee
   21 South 12th Street
   Akron, Pa. 17501
       or
   201-1483 Pembina Hwy.
   Winnipeg, Manitoba R3T 2C8

Books Concerned with World Food Needs:

1. <u>Alternative Celebration Catalog</u>, IV
   Alternatives, 4274 Oaklawn Drive, Jackson, Ms. 39206

2. <u>Bread for the World</u>, Arthur Simon (New York: Paulist Press,
   1975; Grand Rapids, Mich.: Eerdmans, 1975)

3. <u>Diet for a Small Planet</u>, Frances Moore Lappé (New York:
   Ballantine Books, 1975)

4. <u>Enough Is Enough</u>, John V. Taylor (Minneapolis, Mn.:
   Augsburg Publishing House, 1975)

5. <u>Food First</u>, Frances M. Lappé and Joseph Collins (New
   York: Ballantine, 1977)

6. <u>More-with-Less Cookbook</u>, Doris Janzen Longacre
   (Scottdale, Pa.: Herald Press, 1976)

7. <u>Rich Christians in an Age of Hunger</u>, Ronald J. Sider
   (Downers Grove, Ill.: Inter-Varsity Press, 1976)

8. <u>The Twenty-Ninth Day</u>, Lester Brown (New York: Norton, 1978)

9. <u>Living More with Less</u>, Doris Janzen Longacre
   (Scottdale, Pa.: Herald Press, 1980)

Index of Recipes

Index of Recipes

Snacks

♥ With special thanks to...

....our husbands - Jim, Ron, and Don
for their encouragement and love

...Jeanne Rees - a creative cook

...Seho Park - a Korean artist for his
watercolor renditions of the
children's art on the cover and
the recipe division pages

...and our young artist friends:

Colleen Kelly- for her gifted touches throughout the book,
     pages 1, 9, 11, 12, 28, 29, 44, 92, 116, 126, 140, 147, 152, 169
Lynn Walker- front cover
Kim Kramarz - recipe division, pages 33, 133
Lissa Marshall- recipe division, page 69, and pages 25, 76, 84, 100, 130, 131
Cindy Kirkman- recipe division, page 109
Jill Marshall - page 27
John Miller- page 31
Joe Jennings- page 34
Lisa Sommers - page 47
David Treff - page 51
Tracy McClellan- page 56
Suzy Liebert - page 88
Lana Corpuz- page 96
Susie Hunt - page 113
Tami Sharp - page 164

lettering 'n ladybugs   by Marianne Frase

Linda Hunt:

Presently a writing instructor at Spokane Community College and free-lance writer, Linda graduated from the University of Washington. After college, she taught in junior and senior high schools and worked with Young Life, a nondenominational Christian outreach program for teenagers. She also worked for the YWCA while completing a Master's degree at Whitworth College. The parents of three children, she and her husband, Jim, were sensitized to the worldwide importance of personal nutrition when they adopted their son Jeff, a four-year-old Korean child.

Marianne Frase:

During her eighteen years as an elementary school teacher (in the San Francisco Bay Area, Princeton, Atlanta, and Spokane) Marianne has used her "lettering and ladybugs" to enhance the joy of learning for children. A graduate of the University of California at Berkeley, she also has a Master's degree in reading from Whitworth College. She and her husband, Ron, became acutely aware of world food concerns while in Brazil working with the United Presbyterian Church USA mission program. They have two teenage daughters.

Doris Liebert:

After growing up in Calgary, Alberta, Doris attended Seattle Pacific University, where she majored in home economics. While working with Young Life in Pasadena, California, she met her husband, Don, a student at Fuller Seminary. She stayed home for several years while her children were young and gradually earned a Master's degree in early childhood education at Whitworth College. Presently on the faculty of Washington State University, she supervises student teachers. Her kitchen is a neighborhood gathering place, where she enjoys cooking with her three children and all their friends.